Introduction

Envision strolling through the entryway of a house, presently envision that the inside of that house is so clear you could eat off the floor assuming you wished. Then, as you stroll through the house you find that everything is slick and tidy.
There are no toys on the floor, no garments held tight the rear of the love seat, no magazines or lose desk work on the end table. Not dust, hanging in the air.

Then, as you tune in, you can hear repeated heels as they hit the floor- - at the opposite finish of the house. But what gets you about this houses interior is the music that is wafting through the air. Its tune follows you as you advance from one space to another. The sound is old style and it has a quieting impact. Not just on the climate of the actual house, however its occupant's as well.

Entering each room you wonder about the degree of tidiness at which the proprietor declares: Yep, Everything is in its place since everything has a

place.

Now in the event that you will envision strolling through another entryway. The inside of this house is not normal for anything you have at any point seen. Quickly after entering the torrent of sights, sounds and scents hits you the second you stroll in. There are toys extending from one finish of the house to the next. There's somebody's handbag and coat hung across a doorway table which likewise has a blossom plan on it, presently pushed over. Dishes that have been forgotten from the previous evening's late night nibble. Then the scents that hit are a combination of the previous evening's singed supper, the present lunch, aroma and something you can't exactly put your finger on.

In the distance are not repeated heels as in our first situation, however that of beating as though somebody was involving a mallet some place in the house. The separated music you presently hear isn't that of tranquil old style, yet that of drums, guitar, and a shrieking voice so clearly they make your ears hurt and need to run out of the house screaming.

Now let me pose you an inquiry: which climate could you be more agreeable ready? The vast majority of you might have said the main place obviously. But now let me pose another thought for you to ponder. Imagine a scenario in which in the principal house you

put your satchel or coat down and it vanishes out of nowhere placed in an inconspicuous area or more regrettable yet make the whole room wrong and un-kept. In that occasion where it feels awkward you would feel awkward wouldn't you?

Now what might be said about assuming you set your equivalent tote and coat in the subsequent house, you could at no point think that it is in the future. So which spot addresses you and how you live? Which house do you reside in?

While these day to day environments might be outrageous, one marvels is there a fair compromise? I accept there is. Since how you live, where you live, and in what variant you like, tumult or quiet will meaningfully affect your health.

As you keep perusing, I will impart to you players in my past as I figured out how I resided, thought, and kept my home, incredibly impacted others' thought process of me as well as what it meant for my state of mind, usefulness, and health.

In the accompanying sections I will share systems that I have found and started utilizing in my life which has significantly further developed things. I want to believe that they help you as well.

~

My auntie and uncle were inside planners. Other than building custom furnishings or reupholstering existing furnishings, they were asked into homes or workplaces to assist with upgrading entire rooms. This stretched out to display areas too when they lived in Vegas. During the summers I had the option to partake in this experience. Perhaps for that reason I appreciate adjusting my home and watching home improvement shows so a lot, it's in my blood kind of talk. While I don't have the foggiest idea about how Feng

Shui functions, I in all actuality do realize what works (and doesn't work) for me.

After long stretches of investing energy in my aunties and uncles shop, I have changed my methods, styles, and tips to clean sort out and orchestrate my home over the years.

The accompanying parts incorporate what I have found, attempted and arranged into my own style, on the grounds that while all books and articles might have a similar principle objective which is to help you clean and put together you and your space, not these will work for everybody. Pick the ones that are appropriate for you and dispose of the rest since you need to like the framework you decide to the point of continuing to utilize it.

Chapter 1: Clutter-Free Mind

I'm an essayist, and I'm likewise claustrophobic. So stopped or shut in spaces don't bring me solace. That's what i've discovered in the event that the thoughts won't stream, this is on the grounds that there's something in my encompassing region that is awkward, and the main way I will actually want to return to work is spotless something.

However, before each composing project, I clean my work area region so my environmental elements are without messiness. Sounds ordinary right? I anyway attempt and take it farther. I likewise clean any region my eyes might ponder too during my composing time. I do this since anything my eye might meander too while I work should be perfect or I will quit attempting to clean it as opposed to keeping fixed on what I should be doing.

By venture's end in any case, I frequently can't find my work area due to all the messiness that has been assembling and stacking up around me. A portion of those things are, yet not restricted to, books, pens, paper, white out, reference books, and my light. These do exclude my espresso mug, which is an unquestionable requirement have, or the PC on which I use to write.

Now despite the fact that the space my work area sets on is in an open region, the highest points of the work area and its substance sends a gentle instance of tension flowing through my body assuming something is awkward. This might cause alarm since I can't find something when I want it. So I stop to simply revamp the wreck until I'm finished with the task. Since it's completely required it's simply been lost from where it was the point at which I started. So before I start another composing project, I resume one of the many getting sorted out books I have and start with stage one by and by promising to remain coordinated and mess free.

Although I've observed a framework I like and will acquaint you with, I additionally found one more book on association that clears up how for arrange as well as why putting together my home beginnings with me and the manner in which I think and view things.

As I read, I likewise discovered that my reasoning of past and future considerations kept me from the present. That is on the grounds that I was not just reasoning of the previous mishaps I had made, yet additionally future objectives I was attempting to reach. This made me incapable to zero in on NOW.

So in light of the fact that I was zeroing in on things other than whatever was currently before me I was denying myself of the present and hence squandering time.

But assuming you are new to getting sorted out and cleaning up your space and life you might be pondering where on earth do you begin? How do you have at least some idea where to try and start? Since let's be honest: assuming you've perused more than one book, you'll see they all have intriguing and innovative ways of getting and remain organized.

Their styles and approaches might be unique, however they all have similar key beginning stages. Every one of them suggest you start with a schedule as well as day-organizer, a need list, void document envelopes, and a shredder. The rest will fluctuate contingent upon which strategy you pick. But the one thing that may or may not be in these books you pick up is the fact you need persistence to change the way you do things currently.

Now, you might be pondering exactly the way that long it will take to change your reasoning so that remaining coordinated and mess free turns into a habit.
According to specialists it takes between 21 days and 90 days. So about thirty-to-forty redundancies of doing likewise before it turns out to be natural. It simply relying upon the propensity and individual.

Because I have perused somewhere around six books in regards to ways of clearing and wipe mess out of your space and remain coordinated, I have attempted a few of these ideas and have taken pieces and pieces from each book and executed them in my day to day existence to keep coordinated and tranquil for the most part.

See that is the excellence of this framework, in the event that something doesn't work for you, you can change it to fit you. The rest you can let be. There's an extraordinary saying I generally attempt and recollect when I read and rehash these books: "Take what you need and leave the rest." After all observing that works for you is what's truly going on with it, correct? So again utilize the things you can and dispose of the rest.

Next, I love tone, so the one thing I loved about a few of these various frameworks, was the shading and imagination you can join into setting up your system.

Now I'll provide you with a rundown of potential supplies you might require now so you can begin looking for them before we really get to setting up the framework which we will cover in section three. Here are the provisions you will need and that I used to make the system.

- File cabinet
- Shredder File
- folders Filler
- paper
- 3x5 or 4x6 index cards
- 3x5 or 4x6 File box Pens, and pencils

- Pencil sharpener or

- Pencil lead for mechanical pencil

- Binder
- Dividers
- Calendar or day planner
- To do list prioritized
- Three boxes marked keep, give away, or trash
- And numbers to thrift stores once you sort clothes or other things you want to get rid of.

Chapter 2: Where Clutter Collects

Clutter doesn't just gather in our homes; it likewise in our connections, occupations, and thinking. And if we do not rid ourselves of it we will continue to see issues where there should be peace and productivity. Coming up next is the manner by which mess can attack different parts of our lives and how we can manage it.

The primary thing you should do is find exactly the way that you invest and utilize your energy. The creator of Life Simplified recommends you pose yourself two inquiries: The main inquiry: 'Is this my obligation?' and the subsequent inquiry: 'Would I be able to control the issue?' If the solution to both of these is no, this is considered mental clutter.

Another idea is to focus on your timetable. Glynnis Whitwer from I Used To Be So Organized says to figure out which request to focus on your rundowns is to consider five things:

1. Energy level
2. Available time
3. The most earnest deadline
4. Interest level in task
5. Number of insignificant yet fascinating emails

If you're a Christian as I am, ask yourself, 'Is this God's priority or mine?' Once you've identified your goals vs. others goals you have placed on your shoulders, start with number one and move down the list until you've finished.

However, in the event that you don't have the foggiest idea what your objectives might be write down a rundown of five or six regions you wish you had more opportunity to give to. As you do this, remember the endproduct you need to accomplish. Make sure to ask is what you doing drawing you nearer to this objective you have set? Or then again is it removing you from it and in the other direction?

One thing that removes you from your objective, as expressed above, which isn't in your control is mental clutter.

Something else we probably won't consider mind mess is the way we spend our cash. Since we're paid for our time when we work, we should be careful of how we spend that cash once we get it.

It should go for what we need and need, not on things we can live without or unimportant. Since those things don't carry us closer to our goals.

The more I started to investigate this the more I started to learn it is more than keeping a messiness free home and office, it's the way to inside keep mess from us. This incorporates you and what your identity is and what you decide to encircle yourself with.

Another thing that is essential in disposing of messiness, getting and remaining coordinated and achieving your objectives is getting or remaining motivated.

Again assuming you are Christian an incredible method for propelling yourself is to start a recipe called 'petitioning God power'. Furthermore, this framework incorporates prayerize, picturize, and actualize.

Basically implore about your need, picture it and afterward watch as it comes to pass.

Obviously there will be days you are excessively worried, tired, or sick that your inspiration and energy level will be low or non-existent. But if you are truly passionate about what you are doing even when you are not on top of your game, that passion will be there when you get to feeling better.

Just recall genuine inspiration comes from somewhere inside and brings about something you are truly enthusiastic about. So it's not going away.

Chapter 3: A Look At Bad Stress

As I referenced before there are three regions in our lives where mess gather. The principal space is obviously our homes. Where we store the stuff we have, which generally is out of place.

The subsequent region is in our own lives. This incorporates the things we permit to enter it. A portion of these things in our lives might incorporate schedules, ceremonies, and propensities we are utilized to.

The third thing which might be more distressing and harder to dispose of or oversee is with the connections we have.

In this section, we'll zero in on these areas since they are the place where the establishments that make up our lives. And because they're our foundations we must work to keep them strong. The primary thing you ought to do to sort out which of the three regions are the most vulnerable for yourself and needing fix. That is the place where you start. Assuming that you're thinking your house is the place where you're the most fragile, remain tuned. We'll cover that in part four.

The main region we will cover is your life. This comprises of how you handle things whether it's with your work or at home. Anyway as indicated by Mr. Knight not all pressure is awful, regularly stress makes a big difference for us and keeps us pushing ahead. Whenever stress starts to make a negative difference or effect on your wellbeing, is the point at which you really want to make a stride back and check things out. Inclining further toward the great pressure will be talked about later in this book.

We should zero in on what makes us blissful or satisfies our life reason and take out what doesn't.

~

Next is the messiness we have because of our connections. As you take a gander at these connections, inquire as to whether the individuals who are a major part of your life are negative for you. Do they will more often than not have issues in their connections that they share with you as they cry on your shoulder?

Now let me offer one more conversation starter to you. Are there times when individuals come to you wanting a shoulder, once as well as again and again? Or then again have there been times when everything starts to heap on you relating to others and their connections while you are having issues in your own life?

Obviously, this simply adds to issues that you are managing. In the event that you resemble me this main sources you to feel down and discouraged and looking to hide.
However, this can be something worth being thankful for in light of the fact that to hold yourself back from becoming ill, you want to deal with yourself and remain solid. Just turn off and recharge your batteries.

I realize I do. After the entirety of your time is valuable and you ought to attempt to keep yourself certain. Assuming you truly do view your companions or partners as a causes, you might need to see severing associations with these individuals - if you can.

Chapter 4: Clearing The Clutter: Getting Rid Of Stuff

Now that we've viewed at mess in your life as well as connections, we should take a gander at the messiness that gathers in our homes. When you stroll into your house would you say you are over whelmed by what you see the second you stroll in the door?

Are there dirty dishes still in the sink or dishwasher that haven't either been washed or put away if they are clean? Or have you walked into your child's room to find something that could be mistaken for a science project growing in their room? Is there junk mail or outdated magazines lying around? Are there coats not hung up or shoes laying in the pathway just waiting for someone to trip?

What about your timetable? Do you sleep late or miss gatherings and work all together? Do you over plan occasions? Come in late to your youngster's presentation? I can see you I have done likewise. But there is a way to clear the clutter, and make sure your calendar holds the many events your life holds and are scheduled on your calendar and or day planner. Assuming you live on your PC as I do, or have a cell phone, there are electronic schedules that could strike your fancy.

The following thing you need to do is plan time to arrange what you have and to dispense with the articles you might have or have more than one of. This is the point at which you will require three boxes: One for saving one for throwing and the keep going for giving. On the off chance that there is something you don't know of placed it in the keep box until you are certain how you need to manage it.

Do this with each room in the house as well as office. We will examine administrative work in the following part. Whenever you've finished a room, offer yourself a reprieve and award. Particularly on the off chance that a room or the things you're going through are things you have had an enthusiastic connection with.

Once you have experienced each room and have concluded what you wish to keep, throw, or give, begin settling on telephone decisions to associations to see which spot will acknowledge these things and any data you could require. After everything's gone, you start tidying up these rooms including a layer of paint assuming it is necessary.

Now we move to the paper part of wiping out things from your life.

Chapter 5: Getting Rid Of Paper

The following thing we will manage is disposing of the hills of administrative work you might have amassed. I know how simple it is for bill sees, receipts, garbage mail, and whatever else can amass. Even documents which you have duplicates of because you have misplaced the first copy.

The primary thing I took in a couple of years prior, was that on the off chance that it tends to be recovered somewhere else then you don't keep it in your control. Put things such as birth certificates, marriage and death certificates, living wills, social security cards, and any other legal documents that is or may be needed at some point in a safety deposit box.

Other papers that you should deal with are things, for example, youngsters' school souvenirs, report cards, welcoming cards, and whatever else you haven't taken a gander at in 90 days or more.

Now assuming you're a parent and have kept things from consistently your kid or kids has been in school, there might be many things to throw out or settle on a choice on.

The one thing I learned years prior is to deal with each piece of paper just a single time if at all possible.

When we get to how to arrangement your Family and Home fastener in the following section you will see what to do in the event that you in all actuality do have to deal with a piece of paper more than once.

Chapter 6: Setting Up Your Family and Home Binder

Now we move to setting up a family and home folio which will hold different family and home occasions, arrangements and bill installments. This is my main thing since this is the place where you can get innovative and artistic.
According to Pam Young and Peggy Jones, this is the place where you keep everything relating to your family, from birthday events to commemorations from Christmas present plans to garments sizes.

The thought is to never stress over recollecting something since it will be kept in this cover for simple access. You do this with all relatives beginning with you first.
AS guaranteed here is the place where you can put those bits of paper you should deal with at least a time or two, things like bills. After you place the family dividers, you place your schedule. Put the date the bills due on the date due then set the bill in a defensive sheet behind that day. Ensure you set an update a couple of days before the bill is expected. This will give you sufficient opportunity assuming you will mail it. At no point be surprised in the future with past due bills.

Other things that can go into this scratch pad are things like menus, shopping records, duplicates of the family assets in your home for protection purposes.

This is the place where you can likewise add your family task ace rundown. This is extraordinary thought on the off chance that you have youngsters and they have their own errands. Along these lines, they can see precisely when they need to do a task. Then when they really complete that errand, you might put a gold star close to the task on the graph. This is an extraordinary motivator to get the children to do their chores.

Once you wrap up assembling your journal you can then move these things to a 3x5 or 4x6 card likewise shading coded. This is the place where you will start utilizing the card document and list cards I referenced before. You place the month to month divider names first and behind that you place the dated cards, (I needed to make mine I was unable to observe 1-31 in list cards).

The cards marked ABC, you can use for your telephone directory so you can monitor all the significant telephone numbers you have. Keep each number on an alternate card. On each card record a contact name telephone number and

whatever else like birthday, commemoration, or then again if a business the hours and address. Like that assuming you have all the data in a single spot, and on the off chance that you never again have need for that card for reasons unknown, you can undoubtedly dispose of it.

Your card document can likewise hold smaller than normal diary sections. For more data about that I would get a duplicate of the book and find additional astounding things you can add. The thoughts are in a real sense endless.

~

Because of the various styles and shades of file cards, the different things that will go into your card document are endless.

The shading choices they suggest are yellow, pink, blue and white. In spite of the fact that they utilize the white cards for speedy positions, and additionally for writing down fast notes, I isolated those and utilize green for fast positions. That way they are more straightforward to see initially. The yellow cards are for everyday jobs.

Coming up next is an illustration of how you can set up a card with a day to day week by week month to month or every other month errand on it. Select a shading for every class and compose the errand on one side with what amount of time that task could really require, i.e.

Daily/15 minutes/Bathroom

Then, on the reverse side, write down what exactly needs done:

- Scrub toilet, sink and tub
- Sweep and mop floor
- Wipe down mirror and shower door.

You do this with each errand that you have. Assuming you need to skirt a task for a day or week, that is totally fine. Similarly as long as it isn't skipped two times since that will make you fall further behind.

If you're like me and don't want to clean for a lot of time, you can get a

clock and set it for five minutes. Most anybody can clean something for only five minutes. Set the clock and begin cleaning a segment, assuming you finish before the clock goes off, begin another section.

When the clock goes off you will have tidied up a segment of a room that was not perfect five minutes prior, and you will have a feeling of accomplishment

as a result of it. The way in to the folio and card document is to utilize it daily.

Now that you have cleaned your place and set up your binder and card file let's move on to Good stress vs. bad stress.

(If you're keen on more models and clarifications on the best way to utilize the frameworks I've spread out, I urge you to look at the rundown of books in 'References', on the second to last page.)

Chapter 7: Good Stress

We talked momentarily before about what awful pressure can incorporate and what it can mean for you and your body. Presently we investigate how great pressure can help you.

The principal thing I learned was that great pressure hoists your exhibition (1). Great pressure is the something you would rather not be without on the grounds that it keeps you mindful and fixated on what you are doing.

Next, great pressure likewise assists you with remaining stimulated, useful, and centered. The most ideal way to keep a decent anxiety is to observe what your life object is. AS you do this, think about what presents to you the most enthusiasm and satisfaction in your life? What is the one thing that makes you forget about time and keeps limited in on what you are really going after at the present time.

Finding that one thing that you observe enthusiasm for will hold you back from utilizing previous mishaps to drive yourself into accomplishing something since it pays the bills.

Finding your life's motivation additionally helps you not stress over what the following person has on the grounds that you are happy with what you have and who you are.

To summarize this section I will statement from Ben Knight from Organize! The insider facts of an immaculate life: "Genuine inward satisfaction returns from giving and watching others succeed."

Chapter 8: Disciple And Goal Setting

Discipline, defeating hesitation, objective setting, making structure, shutting out time, and testing ourselves, are the thing we will zero in on in the final part of this book. Since you have cleaned up, cleaned, set up a framework to keep everything all together, you presently need to start to retrain yourselves so you don't fall once again into your old habits.

Because the manner in which we live has been the aftereffect of how sponsors, companions, and even family have affected our lives, we can not out of nowhere change. It will require some investment. So the principal thing we want to do is to change our discipline. But first we may need to understand what disciple is and it is a moral and mental training. Or then again retraining in our case.

I consider retraining ourselves to be taking stock of our assets and shortcomings. While we can praise our assets, we really want to sort out some way to transform our shortcomings into strengths.

An illustration of a shortcoming would be not taking care of something after we have utilized it, or not doing the evening dishes and leaving them until morning. I don't know about you but I am not a morning person, so the last thing I want to do is dishes before coffee.

Another shortcoming we might have is allowing others to talk us into something we don't need. Whether it's something special to do, purchase or go. One reason we permit this to happen is laziness.

If we permit this to occur or proceed with this gives our self image a shock and permits cynicism to flourish and decrease what our identity is or could be assuming that we persevered. This next part is my number one, in light of the fact that as an essayist, it's something I do sooner or later and that is to work out a strategy or outline.

Write out the things you wish to achieve in your life. Incorporate your time period and what it resembles. Then the way that long it might take to get these things done. This way when you end up getting sidetracked you have something to check out and allude to.

An expression of watchfulness while making your objectives and that is to not tell anybody. I realized this firsthand on the grounds that when I told somebody, I frequently did not complete or arrive at my objective due to the doubters I ran into. On the off chance that you really do choose to tell somebody, and they answer with an absence of help and support there are a few things you can do. To begin with, surrender and disregard your objectives. Second, get new companions, and never again inform others regarding your objectives and progress. Or then again third, toss your shoulders back, take a full breath, observe new companions and push ahead telling nobody you doing. But if you are retraining yourself, or are new to creating positive, good stressed events, you may not know where to begin.

Chapter 9: Making The Choice

The principal thing you want to do is decide that changing is what you need to do. And it will be for the better. The following thing is understanding that change won't occur all of a sudden. That is on the grounds that it took you years to get where you are presently. So it will require some investment to steer your life for the better.

Once you have decided to redirect your life you ought to add these means to your framework under every objective that you past plan.

Remember that when you begin making transforms, overpowering yourself by laying out your objectives too high is significant not. Also set them to low, or you will get exhausted. You need to challenge yourself so you can move forward to the subsequent stage and advance your progress.

To accomplish this ensure your plans for the day are in little lumps. Setting our sights to high first thing is a certain fire method for setting us up for disappointment. So in the event that we believe these objectives and changes should produce results and stick, we really want to begin slow and with more modest more attainable goals.

According to specialists it requires somewhere around 90 days for another propensity to become programmed and consequently a daily practice. Try not to take a gander at the outcome yet rather take a gander at each undertaking that will push you ahead to the last goal.

While you are on this new excursion there will be days where you will be up and days you will be down, and perhaps tested or potentially feel crushed. When this does happen it is important to stay positive and optimistic, because if you think of the glass half full you are more likely to stay moving forward and making things happen.

Chapter 10: Stop Procrastination

Now we move to lingering. This is postponing until tomorrow what you ought to do now. On the off chance that you're not cautious this can be a long lasting fight. One method for halting stalling, notwithstanding, is to make structure in your life.

If this is the kind of thing new you are endeavoring, that little voice you have inside won't quit attempting to inspire you to stop what you are at present doing. But in order to make the change, you must start somewhere, anywhere. So you can keep on pushing ahead as new propensities occur. (1)

One extraordinary method for keeping yourself on course and not feel you are distant from everyone else, is a care group or amigo, to roll out this incredible improvement with you. Having an amigo complete three things, they can 1) assist with keeping you inspired, or 2) root for you when you are drawing near to the end goal, or cheer you up when you are having inconvenience and feel defeated.

Another thing that helps ward of hesitation is completing what you start. By doing this it will provide you with a feeling of achievement. At the point when you have gotten done with a venture that had been begun it is simply right to remunerate yourself since that was getting and going on with something that might have been difficult for you to do in any case, which might have been the explanation you halted in the first place.

The way to beginning and completing something is to defined reasonable objectives regardless. Becoming overextended, resembles the colloquialism your eyes were greater than your stomach.   Big dreams are incredible, yet to own them and not quit makes sensible strides and achievements. This will assist you with arriving at little objectives as you keep on climbing the means to success.

After all gnawing off more that you can bite is making awful pressure and that isn't the thing you are making progress toward anymore.

Chapter 11: What A Minimalist Is

So far we have examined cleaning mess off of our lives, recovering command over the long run, cash, and assets, managing hesitation, and found out about objective setting, and discipline, we'll currently dive into what this is paving the way to and means.

It implies you're leaving on a better approach for living and a better approach for seeing your life. Yet again it's clearing a path so you can track down your genuine's motivation and start to appreciate living, presently more tranquil promotion more mess free. Are you game? Here we go:

According to Life Simplified, an existence of mineralization is "a shift of eliminating interruptions and things from your life that have practically no worth and supplanting them with things or exercises that give you delight and value."

Now in the wake of perusing the definition who would have no desire to jump aboard to do that. After all prior didn't we see our time was cash, so cash so hence it was valuable? To work at putting things in our experience that will add worth and delight? So why isn't that right? Since for one its diligent effort to change what our identity is, and two on the off chance that we decide to transform we should change our attitude and thinking. Since being moderate isn't killing mess and individuals or even living essentially. It's a 180 degree change in our life, thinking and acting.

To envision what it resembles think about what setting up camp is like. You don't get together your entire house, you take exactly what you really want: Bedding food, cookware, garments, tent, fishing supplies, and perhaps a book or composing diary and pen. That is all there is to it. You don't take the PC machines printer sofa or different things you own.

Being a moderate is a way of life change that keeps you aware of things the entire day. A lifestyle is everlastingly a piece of you and who you are.

As I read more about what being a moderate is, I started to see pieces of me in this lifestyle. Have you at any point felt you might have been brought into the world in some unacceptable time? I have. I have generally imagined

myself being content during the little house on the grassland, or Walton's, the straightforward lifestyle. Because
during that time there wasn't every one of the gismos and devices that we have now, no commercials to inspire us to purchase the best in class thing. However, more on that later.

During that time, families not just buckled down for their cash which they spent on things they required needed as well as they likewise invested energy with loved ones. Life was extremely straightforward however according to my perspective it was additionally practical.

As you will find in the following parts we make being reasonable one stride farther as we investigate the idea of being content.

Chapter 12: Are You Content?

As we move into the subsequent stage of turning into a moderate, you should pose the inquiry: Am I content?

In the New Testament of the Holy Bible, we see that Paul discusses how he has figured out how to be content. Presently I couldn't say whether he is viewed as a moderate, however that's what I know whether he can get it done, it tends to be finished. But now you may be asking how can it be accomplished? How can I become content with what I have?

What number of us contrast ourselves as well as other people or are encircled by the individuals who contrast themselves as well as other people concerning what their identity is, what they have, or how they live?

What we see is that we (or they) are perpetually discontent with exactly what our identity is. But what we must remember is that there will always be someone richer, happier, smarter, skinnier, or any other thing we can think of.

The main individual you ought to be preferable over is the sort of person you were yesterday. There is just a single you and that assertion alone makes you remarkable and exceptional. Perhaps the inquiry we ought to present isn't am I content, however would someone say someone is seeing me wanting to be me?

Chapter 13: Purpose, Practice, and People

Now we come to the inquiry: How would we live with reason? Indeed, there are three things we should do, known as the 3 P's.

The first is track down your motivation. Do you have a calling? What is something you are attempting to achieve or accomplish that would mean something?

If you're not accomplishing something pushing you one stride ahead, you might observe your life loaded up with uneasiness and stress.

The subsequent thing: you want to pursue building solid routines that will push you ahead, instead of in reverse. Since going in reverse or stopping is considered a squandered day.

Finally, the third thing you should zero in on is individuals. What sort of individuals would you say you are encircle yourself with? Are they individuals who will support and help you, or are they cynics who will contrarily disrupt your endeavors when we attempt to achieve something?

Chapter 14: Valuing Your Money and Time

Next, we take a gander at the cash you've gotten due to your important time. Planning and the moderate are connected, in light of the fact that you will start to see and zero in on purchasing just things that give you joy, as well as have a need. This eliminates purchasing something the most current thing particularly when the old thing actually works. Or then again something unimportant as it hangs close to the register.

Spending cash on things we don't actually require makes us go under water and prompt us to get from bucket to pay peter. We never appear excel in light of the fact that we are continuously attempting to get up to speed. To assist with controlling mess a moderate ought to start eliminating one thing prior to acquiring something new.

Life is too short to even think about squandering one second accomplishing something pointless, inefficient, ineffective, or doesn't give us joy or satisfaction. This is additionally how a moderate thinks.

Since we have put esteem on cash while purchasing something, shouldn't we likewise put that equivalent worth on us and our time? As expressed above life is too valuable to even think about squandering a life on accomplishing something we despise, as or isn't pleasurable. Why then don't we put that equivalent worth on our positions? Or then again more regrettable yet for what reason do we permit others to downgrade us and our time and additionally skills?

Obviously, in this economy it ought to be valid we ought to be content to have business, it is likewise a fact that we shouldn't allow others to cheapen us and burn through the time we have given them.

Each of us has an ability and take on a place that might be not as much as the thing we are searching for, we ought to do everything and make a move to do all that can be expected out of the open door we are given.

If we work independently and offering an expertise at a cost, we shouldn't put a lower cost on our time since we might not have the experience as others might have. What you proposition might be of worth to somebody that another organization doesn't offer. So don't put a lower esteem on your time and experience since you don't figure you can compete.

Chapter 15 - Ways We Are Targeted

Now, we move to better ways of expenditure your cash, regardless of the endeavors by publicists to inspire you to spend your cash on their item or administration. When you start to begin putting a worth on your cash, this is the very time you will observe that you may more consideration regarding these promotion's and start to see exactly how simple to lose your money, on the off chance that you're not careful.

Unfortunately you can't escape from them- - advertisements are they are all over. They are the things that interfere with your TV show (and typically exactly at that crucial point in time), to the spring up that is normally positioned perfectly focused of a website page you are visiting. They are even on boards you pass when you are on a family drive toward the end of the week. Shoot they are even in our papers and what most consider garbage mail.

However, individuals pursue the open door when these promotions come on during a show to make a beeline for the kitchen, do dishes (your conceivable brief cleaning meeting), go to the restroom, or do anything that removes you from the TV for that time span. Regardless of whether you notice them deliberately they stick in your sub-conscience very much like the tune from Disneyland that you can't escape your head for days, weeks or months after you leave there. Plugs do it similarly with the rings that are played during the commercial.

So, how do promoters guide you into purchasing their item as well as administration? A few publicists even objective our youngsters. They'll get a youngster's attention and consideration. Try not to accept me take your kid shopping one day and watch as you stroll down the cereal walkway. Watch how they go after and need the cereal with the most brilliant hued logos or characters.

These publicists know the least demanding method for inspiring us to purchase something or head off to some place is frequently through our kids. Presently in the wake of perusing that you might ask yourself how low they will go, as to focus on our kids. But as the saying goes, it's not personal, It's only business.

As a moderate we currently have a better approaches for contemplating what to purchase or administrations we pick. Moving your reasoning will compel you to truly check out and see exactly the way that an organization convince you to purchase their item and remain faithful to them. This is frequently on the grounds that you are snared to that product.

Chapter 16: Kissing Debt Good-Bye

We see it constantly, a name brand right close to an off brand. One more costly than the following yet both contain the very same item. So what is the distinction between whether you get one over the other? Most frequently it's basically on the grounds that you know a name over the other, your family has been faithful to that item. Or then again like me you have become acclimated to one taste or another.

Before you purchase any item, it is critical to investigate that item to see which item is ideal. It shouldn't exactly be an issue of value, it ought to truly be an issue of nature of the item, assuming it is the more costly sort, is it will merit the cash, is it an item that is going to endure or is it will require supplanting since it is sub-par and made of terrible quality material. All things considered, shouldn't the items and administrations you purchase keep going as long as possible?

Lastly, we will examine motivation purchasing as opposed to planning for something we need. Motivation purchasing is seeing something and getting it now. Impulse buying is seeing something and getting it now. That is the point at which we start to put something aside for it whether it's this month or a later time.

This additionally gives us time for the love or captivation to wear off and we can truly started to ponder if we want that thing however much we thought we did.

It likewise allows us an opportunity to check in with our accomplices on the off chance that we want to so different issues don't emerge because of an item that got our attention. In the event that it's something we actually need, we can put something aside for itself and anticipate it sometime in the future.

Chapter 17: Conclusion

Over the beyond sixteen sections, we've taken a gander at different ways of disposing of messiness by cleaning our homes, as well as found that messiness isn't just stuff, yet can be issues that we manage that brings us disappointment, stress and inconvenience in our lives. We figured out how to dispose of that messiness or keep up with it in a more solid manner, we then perceived how to set up a family note pad framework which assists us with keeping everything significant in one spot so we remember or lose anything, as well as dispose of copy records so we can dispose of the paper that channels into our lives daily.

We took in the distinction between great pressure and awful. And that while we want to get rid of bad stress because of our health, we also learned that good stress is a good thing and is something we don't want to be without.

We saw that to address a propensity it requires some investment and tolerance despite the fact that we believe it should happen overnight.

We found ways we can break huge family projects into more modest pieces so we are not overpowered. As we proceeded with we saw that our time is cash and both ought to be esteemed. That we ought to esteem our time since we are interesting and special.

We saw that contrasting ourselves as well as other people isn't something that we ought to do on the grounds that regularly that doesn't make us blissful or content in the end.

We additionally discovered that our cash ought to be spent admirably and that when we shop we ought to search for the best deals we can regardless of whether that item isn't a name brand.

Finally, we discovered that once we settle on a choice to be a moderate that we will be enticed to return to purchasing what we need when we need and we want to remain firm and remain consistent with our most current method of life.

One thing I learned was that it is a lot easier to buddy up and have support while I am making a life altering decision because there will be naysayers and if I am not careful I will revert back to who I was before and become depressed and fall right back into the lifestyle I was working so hard to change.